The WONDERFUL WAY that BABIES ARE MADE

Larry Christenson

The WONDERFUL WAY that BABIES ARE MADE

Illustrated by Dwight Walles

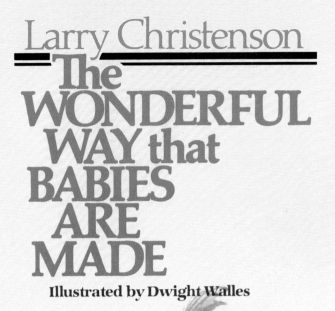

BETHANY HOUSE PUBLISHERS
MINNEAPOLIS, MINNESOTA 55438
A Division of Bethany Fellowship, Inc

Published by Bethany House Publishers
A Division of Bethany Fellowship, Inc.
6820 Auto Club Road, Minneapolis, Minn. 55438

Printed in the United States of America

Library of Congress Cataloging in Publication Data

Christenson, Larry, 1928-
    The wonderful way that babies are made.

    Summary: Presents in poetry and from a Christian view-
point how God created the living things upon the earth so they
could reproduce their own kind—including people.
    1. Sex—Religious aspects—Christianity—Juvenile literature. 2.
Sex instruction for children. [1. Sex—Religious aspects—
Christianity. 2. Sex instruction for children]
I. Walles, Dwight, ill. II. Title.
BT708.C45   1982   649'.65   82-12813
ISBN 0-87123-627-3

FOREWORD TO PARENTS

First, a word about the ones this book is written for. We had two pictures in mind as we prepared it:

* *A parent reading the book aloud to a small child.*
  The illustrations and the large-print verse are designed for small children, ages 3-8.
* *An older child reading the book to himself.*
  The smaller-print paragraphs on each page present additional material for older children, ages 9-14. These also can be read with a parent, if this method is preferable.

Then a word about our way of presenting the story of human sexuality and reproduction: We have attempted to be open and direct with the children without resorting to a "clinical" or "scientific" approach. A child's first need is not a blizzard of scientific information, but *help in shaping a basic attitude toward human sexuality.*

Our hope is that parents can use this book as a tool to help pass on to their children an attitude of joy and wonder in God's gift of life and sexuality. We have set the story against the backdrop of creation, so that from the very beginning a child's understanding of sex will be linked in a positive way to belief in God. Next, we have set it in the context of the family, so that a child's thoughts about "making love" and "having babies" will be associated with the warmth and stability of a Christian home.

A book like this would not have been written a few years ago. The old idea of sex education was to trust the biology textbooks to give children the "facts," then leave them on their own to figure out feelings and attitude. But the *fact* is that feelings and attitude lie at the heart of what Christian sex education ought to be. What good is there in handing children a batch of so-called facts if we leave them guessing about the thing that interests them most—the feelings and attitude, the relationships and emotions? And, more particularly, those of their own parents?

If we do not share with our children the wonderful way that babies are made, they will pick up this information elsewhere, and probably in a distorted fashion. Why let secular society shape the attitudes of our children in so important an area of life? God's way is better: let them receive it from their parents!

This book is a point of contact with your child, a place to begin in presenting the information, the feelings, the attitude which you as a parent would like to share.

Larry Christenson

Here's something wonderful;
Come, look and see—
Father and Mother
   With a *brand-new Baby!*

Have you ever seen a Western
with a lot of tough guys?
Somewhere in the middle of the story
a baby is born,
and suddenly the tough guys get quiet and tender.
It's mysterious and wonderful
when a new baby comes into the world.
There's something about a baby
that tugs even on a tough guy's heartstrings.

Mother thinks
Baby's so wonderful;

Father says so too.

Baby says,
"Ooo-oo-Boop-a-boo!"

Maybe that means wonderful too!

A mother and a father sometimes act as though their new baby
is the most terrific baby that ever was born.
Of course they don't *really* think that;
but when a baby is born into a family,
it *is* something wonderful and special.

It's supposed to be like that.
A new baby needs to feel that it is special—
specially loved, specially wanted.

Sometimes, when a new baby comes into a family,
older brothers and sisters think,
"That baby is nothing but a *bother*!
It's all Mom and Dad have time for anymore!"

It's natural to think that way at first
because, well, new babies *do* take a lot of time and attention.
But as a baby gets a little older,
you find out that it can be nice
to have a new brother or sister in the family.
God meant it to be that way.

Just look at the size of his fingers and toes!
Isn't he a tiny little tot?
But did you know, when he started to grow,
He was tinier even than this tiny dot ➝ · ?

We often say that a baby's life begins when it's born.
But, actually, a baby's life begins
almost a year before it's born.
The way it happens is one of the most wonderful
and interesting things in all God's world!

How *do* little babies start to grow?
Isn't that something everyone ought to know?

If you liked cars, you'd probably
want to find out how they are made.
If you wanted to be a nurse, or an explorer, or a teacher,
you'd like a book that told you how someone gets to be such a person.
It's interesting to learn how things are made or how they happen.

Learning how babies are made is especially interesting because,
well, maybe because all of us were once babies ourselves.
And many of us become fathers and mothers when we grow up.
So learning about babies is really
learning something important about ourselves.

The pictures and big print in this book
are to help the smaller children.
When someone reads it to them,
they can learn important things about
Fathers and Mothers and Babies.

Some of you are older.
You can read for yourself.
This smaller print is for you.
The pictures and the big print
will start you out on an idea.
Then you can read this smaller print.
It will tell you more things that you want to know,
because you are older and can understand
more than small children can.

If *you* want to know,
Come, listen and look,

For that is the story
In this little book.

It's the wonderful story of

THE WONDERFUL WAY

THAT BABIES ARE MADE!

Maybe you already know something about how babies are made.
But if you read all the way through this book,
you may learn some things you didn't know before.

Of course, there's much more to know
than is written in this book.
The book is just a beginning.
As more thoughts and questions
come to your mind, you can talk with your parents.
It's natural to talk to your parents
when you're learning
about how babies are made
and what it means to be a Father or a Mother,
because you're all a family together.

It's not something you talk about with just anybody.
It's special. It's *family* talk!

God planned it all out in a wonderful way.
That is what this book is about:
God's wonderful plan for
Fathers . . . and Mothers . . . and Babies!

Now, to make something fine
    there must first be a Maker;
And the Maker of *all* things
    is God, the Creator.
So what better place
    to begin our story
Than with Him who planned it,
    the God of glory?

God made many wonderful things
    in His wonderful world—

    God made daytime and nighttime,
        the moon and the sun;
    He made stars in the heavens
        where before there were none.
    He made rivers that lazily
        curve through the land;
    He made mountains of granite and
        deserts of sand.

Sometimes it's easier to understand something
if we step back and see a "bigger picture."
For instance, if you put your nose right up against a painting,
you might see only a blob of brown color.
But if you step back, you may discover
that it's a picture of a beautiful tree,
and the brown part is its trunk.

Before we see how babies are made
and how they come into the world,
let's step back and look at the big picture.
Let's think about all the things God has made.
He certainly didn't run out of ideas when He created the world!

After He made the sun and the moon and the stars,
After He made the whole wonderful earth,
God made all kinds of *living things* to be upon
   the earth.

He made turtles
   and turnips
   and tigers
   and trees.

He made barley
   and beetles
   and badgers
   and bees.

"Life" is a great mystery.
We can recognize living things
and describe them.
We can write poems
and songs about them.
But nobody can explain what life itself is,
not even the greatest scientist.

If we look around
(and really open our eyes!),
we can't help saying,
"What a great Creator our God is!"

Last of all, God made *people.*

He wanted something quite different
  than rivers or seas,
Different than animals, birds, or trees;
Different than flowers or fish or sod—
He wanted something to be in the image of God!

He wanted something to be—well, to be like himself,
Not something to paint and put up on a shelf;
But someone like Him who could think and plan,
And that was when He made *Woman and Man.*

The Bible tells us that after God had created everything else,
He created a man and a woman.
They were the first husband and wife on the earth.
The world was their home,
and the animals were their friends.

But they were different than the animals,
because God made them to be like himself.
That doesn't mean that they *looked* like God,
because nobody knows what God looks like.
But He gave them minds so they could think,
and that made them like Him,
for God is a great Thinker.
He gave them a heart that could feel things
like love and tenderness and beauty;
that made them like Him,
for God has a great Heart.
He gave them a will that could choose to do the right thing,
and that made them like Him too,
for God always does what is right.

God thought about all these things He had made—
He saw eagles with feathers
And beavers with fur,
Lions that roared
And cats that could purr.

He saw thousands of fish
That swim in the seas,
And monkeys that swing
By their tails in the trees.

He saw spotted giraffes
That stretch up so tall,
And the Woman and Man
That He loved best of all.

It's good, sometimes,
to stop and think
about the wonderful things God has made.
It helps us remember
that He is the One who made *everything*,
and that when He makes something,
He has a wonderful plan for it.

He has a wonderful plan for *you*.

**After six days of making,
God rested a day;
The angels were waiting
to hear what He'd say.
He decided He'd made
all the things that He should;
He looked it all over
and said *it was good!***

Have you ever tried to fix something,
and the more you tried
the worse it got?
Then you went back
and read the directions and exclaimed,
"Oh, *that's* the way it's supposed to go!"
When you understand how something
is planned and made, it makes more sense.

It's that way with the things God has made.
When we understand how He meant them to work,
then we can say the same thing He says in the Bible:
"It is very good!"

One of the good things God created
was a plan for making new living things,
including babies.

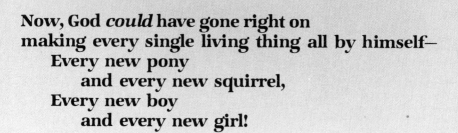

Now, God *could* have gone right on
making every single living thing all by himself—
    Every new pony
        and every new squirrel,
    Every new boy
        and every new girl!

If a man makes tables for a living,
every time someone orders a new table,
he has to build it for them.
God *could* have done that with living things.

He made the first living things,
and He could have gone right on doing it that way.
He could have made thousands and thousands of people all at once.
But we know, of course,
that He didn't do it that way.
He decided to do it differently.

**God decided to do something *wonderful*—
He decided to let every living thing
    help Him make more living things!**

**Raccoons could help Him make raccoons,
Potatoes could help Him make potatoes,
Roses would help Him make more roses,
*And people would help Him make more people!***

Living things make new living things
that are just like themselves.
Wouldn't it be funny
If everything was all mixed up
and you never knew
what kind of new life would get made?
If a tree would drop its seed into the ground,
and start a baby rabbit growing?
Or a fish would lay eggs,
and start a potato growing?
Or a monkey would start a person growing?

But that isn't the way God did it.
He said, "Every living thing
shall make its own kind of life."

**Have you ever wondered how living things do this?
Well, they give a part of themselves
    to get a new life started.**

To start a tree you know that we need
The part of a tree that we call a *seed*.
A bird starts from something not very big,
Something a bird lays that we call an *egg*.

To tell about this we use a word—
It's the same for a bear as it is for a bird,
The same for a goose as it is for a moose—
The word we use is "re-pro-duce."

"Reproduce" is a big long word,
But its meaning is not at all absurd;
It just means to make something quite like you,
Except that it's smaller when it's brand new.

All living things have this wonderful power
To reproduce what they themselves are.
It's the way God planned for new life to start,
It's something in which all living things
        have a part.

        So let's say it again
        And put our brains to use:
        "All living things
        Re-pro-duce!"

God gave every living thing a way to reproduce itself.

They do it by giving a part of themselves.
It doesn't hurt to give it because that's what it's made for.

A big tree gives part of itself to start a new tree growing.
At a certain time of the year—
the time when it's best for new trees to get started—
the big tree drops its seeds to the ground.
When the little seed feels the warm earth around it,
something inside the seed stirs to life and begins to grow.
It's very tiny at first,
but one day it will be a full-sized tree;
and then it will give seeds too, so more new trees can start growing.

We're so used to seeing this happen
that we don't stop to think how wonderful it is.
What is it inside a seed that makes it able to start a new tree growing?
No one can explain it.
It's one of God's wonderful secrets.

For most living things,
it takes *two* of them to reproduce.
It takes a FATHER and a MOTHER—

It takes a Father Horse and a Mother Horse
   to start a Baby Horse.
And it takes a Father Lion and a Mother Lion
   to start a Baby Lion, of course!

And who starts a new baby growing?
That's easy to say—
Father and Mother!
It's God's wonderful way.

A Father gives a special part of himself,
And a Mother gives a special part of herself
   to start a new little baby growing—

   Inside a Father is something called a sperm.
   It has a tail in back so it can swim and turn.
   It's a little bit flat, but it's shaped like a ball,
   And it's very very very very very very small!

   Inside a Mother is something called an egg,
   And like the sperm it's not very big.
   But, believe it or not, from these two little parts
   The life of a brand-new Baby starts!

A father's sperm and a mother's egg
are two of the most amazing things God ever made.
They're so tiny that you can't even see them unless you have a microscope.
And yet they carry more information in them than a computer!
All the different things about the baby are carried
as "information" or "instructions" in the sperm and the egg—
the color its hair will be, whether it will be a boy or a girl,
how tall it will grow up to be, the shape of its chin,
the color of its eyes, whether it will be athletic
or musical or artistic or mechanical.
All of that information, and much more,
is stored in the tiny sperm and egg.
That's the "part of themselves" that a father and a mother give
to start a new little baby growing!

When a sperm from the Father comes together
with an egg from the Mother, a new Baby starts to grow,
And God made a wonderful way for the Father's sperm
and the Mother's egg to come together.
It's something Father and Mother do
    that is called "making love."

When Husbands and Wives make love together,
They kiss and touch and lie close to each other;
For God made their bodies to fit together
So the sperm from the Father can swim into the
    Mother.

Making love was a wonderful part of God's plan
When He made the very first Woman and Man.
It's His beautiful gift just for Husbands and Wives
To bring them happiness all of their lives.

It's not something they talk about like news
    or the weather,
This wonderful way Husbands and Wives
    come together;
It's special and private, something all their own,
Something they do when they're all alone.

"Making love" is one of the wonderful things God planned for husbands and wives.
It's something He made especially for them.
He made their bodies so they would find enjoyment with one another
when they make love.

When a Husband and Wife make love
and bring their bodies so close that they fit together,
it is called "intercourse,"
which means "two things coming together."
The part of the Husband called his "penis,"
which is between his legs,
fits into his wife's "vagina,"
which is between her legs.
That is the place their bodies fit together
when they have intercourse.

Intercourse is a very special and wonderful experience
that a husband and wife share with each other.
It gives them pleasurable feelings in their bodies,
and a sense of love and closeness to each other.

Now husbands and wives don't have intercourse
every time they kiss each other!
Intercourse is something very private,
something they do only when they're alone,
but not *every* time they are alone, of course.

When they have intercourse,
the sperm from the father
can swim into the mother.
A baby doesn't start growing every time
they have intercourse,
because the Mother's body releases a new egg
only once a month.
If there is no egg ready to unite with the sperm
when they have intercourse,
no baby will start growing.

Because intercourse is so pleasant,
sometimes people who are not married to each other want to do it;
but the Bible tells us that it is wrong for people to have intercourse
if they are not married to each other.

Making love the way husbands and wives do
is pleasant and wonderful,
for God made it that way.
But it is something He planned *only for husbands and wives.*
It is a special gift to help them build a strong, loving home,
and a place where new babies can be received and taken care of.

When you have intercourse,
you give yourself in a very special way to the other person.
God says that we are to give ourselves in this way
only if we are married to the other person.
It is a gift God made only for people who are married to each other.
It is a serious sin for people to have intercourse
if they are not married to each other.
It is like taking something that does not belong to you.

**What happens when a sperm from the Father
comes together with an egg from the Mother?**

**When a sperm finds an egg,
The two join together,
And a Baby starts to grow
Right inside the Mother!**

**For inside the mother
There's a special place
for a Baby to grow
Where it's warm and safe.**

It's a little place right next to her tummy
That doesn't even show on her figure;
But when a baby starts growing inside,

Then Mommy gets bigger and Bigger and BIGGER!

Inside a Mother, a little below her waist,
is a place where
a new baby begins its life.
It is called her "uterus," or "womb."
When a baby starts to grow
inside its Mother,
we say that she is "pregnant."
Of course the baby is very,
very tiny to begin with.
The Mother scarcely notices it at first.
But after a few weeks have gone by,
she begins to feel this new
little life inside her.

**Do you know how long a
baby grows inside its mother?** *Nine months.*

**In that warm place it grows and grows,
It grows its fingers and grows its toes,
It grows its nose.
(But it doesn't grow clothes!)**

A baby that's tinier than a dot
couldn't live out in the world right away.
It needs time for its brain
and heart and lungs
and all its other parts to grow and develop.

During those nine months, the tiny little baby
(that began when the father's sperm
and the mother's egg came together)
has a chance to grow and develop
until it weighs about seven pounds,
and is almost 20 inches long.

**And then comes the day, the wonderful day,
when the baby comes out into the world—**

**God made an opening in the Mother's body
So the Baby can come out when the time is
    ready;
It leaves that place, so nice and warm,
And comes out in the world on the day it is *born*!**

A mother's body is wonderfully made for giving birth to a baby.
When it is time for the baby to be born,
powerful muscles inside the mother
begin to push the baby from the womb
out through the vagina and into the world.
When this begins,
we say that the mother is in "labor."
"Labor" usually lasts for several hours
and it causes some pain
because the mother's body has to stretch a lot
in order for the baby to get out.
But when it's over, the mother is happy
because she has a baby to love and take care of.

Here's something interesting to think about:
a year after a baby is born
it has its first birthday,
and we say, "Baby is one year old!"
But really, the baby is almost *two* years old,
counting the time it lived inside its mother.

(In China a baby is counted one year old on the day it is born.
So if you were nine years old
and met someone from China who said, "I'm ten years old,"
you would actually be the same age.)

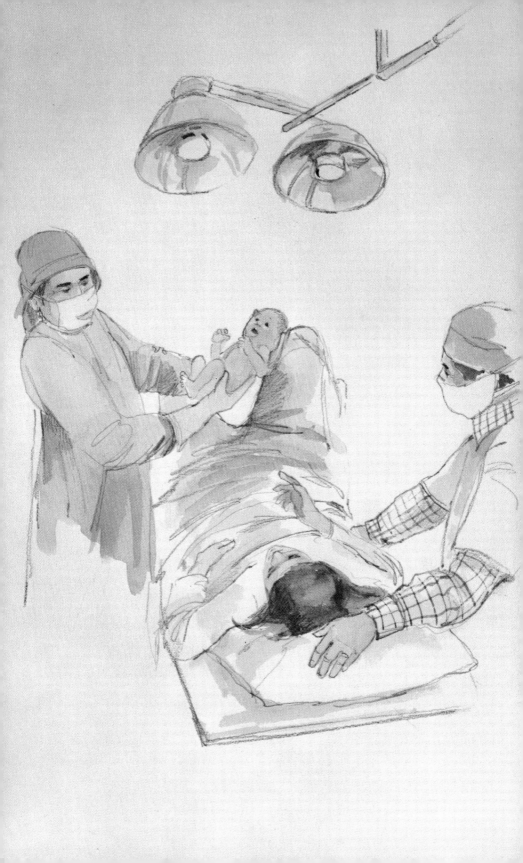

When a Baby is born it needs lots of care;
It needs lots of love, it needs lots of prayer,
It needs food and clothes, and other things too—
And that's the job God gave *Parents* to do!

Having a baby is one of the most important things
that happens on earth.
Just think of it:
In 25 or 30 years that baby will be grown up
and have important responsibilities.
It may even have children of its own.
The babies of today
are the adults of tomorrow!

And who prepares them for their responsibilities?
Parents.
God has entrusted
the training of the next generation to parents.
It's a tremendous privilege
and a great responsibility.

Isn't it wonderful that God gives children parents?

Because what little baby
Is ready at birth
To do all the things
That we do on earth?

It can't change its clothes,
And it can't build a house;
It can't bake a cake,
And it can't catch a mouse!

It needs parents to love it and give it a hug;
It needs parents to show how to vacuum a rug.
It needs parents to teach it the right way to live,
And when things go wrong, how to forgive.

Have you ever thought about all the things
parents do for their children?
Sometimes children get angry
because they can't have something they want
or do something they want to do.
At times like that
parents can seem pretty unreasonable to a child!

But think of all the things
that God expects parents to do for the children
He has given them to take care of:
They must see that the child gets the right kind of food
so that it will grow up strong and healthy,
buy clothes for it,
take it to the doctor and dentist,
send it to school,
teach it the difference between right and wrong,
show it how to do all kinds of different things—
it's enough to make your head swim!

Here's something to think about:
What kind of a parent
are *you* going to be when you grow up?
What kind of things are you going to teach your children?

What kind of rules are you going to have for them?
What are you going to do
when they want to do something that is dangerous or impossible?
What are you going to do
when you tell them to do something
and they don't do it?
Think about it:
*What kind of parent would you like to be
when you have children of your own?*

What kind of parent do you think *God* wants you to be?
That's the real question, isn't it?
That's the question your own parents have to look at.
Because who is the boss of parents?
God is!
We all belong to Him.
Children belong to Him,
and parents belong to Him too.
He wants parents to raise children His way,
the way He tells us about in the Bible.

Now, here's something special to think about:
Suppose that a Father and Mother couldn't
take care of a child for some reason.
One of the wonderful things that can happen then
is that *another* Father and Mother take that child
and become its parents.
This is called being *adopted.*

When a child is adopted
It finds a new home,
With parents who love it
and call it their own.

Sometimes a child loses its father or mother.
Maybe they died before the child was grown,
or maybe they can't take care of the child,
or are not in the home for some reason.
God may provide for someone else to become the child's parents.
We call this being *adopted*.
That means that the new parents take the child into their home
and the child becomes a member of their family.
Even though they didn't have the child themselves,
they become the child's new parents,
and they love it
and take care of it
because it becomes their own child.

**To be adopted
Is not at all new,
For our Lord Jesus
Was adopted too.**

We sometimes forget that Jesus was adopted.
He was adopted by Joseph.

Jesus was born in a very special way.
God sent an angel to Mary,
who was going to become Jesus' mother.
The angel told Mary that she was going to have a baby,
but the baby would not have a father here on earth.

How could that happen?
God did something special, a *miracle*.

Jesus was born in a special way:
An angel announced it to Mary one day.
He said, "You'll be the Mother of God's own Son."
She trusted his words and said, "Let it be done."

The Baby that started to grow inside her
Was a Baby that had no human father.
It was God's special way to send His Son to earth;
It's a miracle we call, "the Virgin Birth."

Mary was a *virgin*.
A virgin is someone who is not married
and has never come together with a man
in the special way that husbands and wives come together.
God did something special in the Virgin Mary.
God's Holy Spirit caused one of the tiny little eggs inside of Mary
to begin growing into a baby.

When the baby was born they named Him *Jesus*,
for that was the name the angel had told them to give the baby.
The name "Jesus" means "Saviour."
God sent Jesus to be our Saviour—to defeat the devil
and break the power of sin and death, so we could become children of God.

The devil and sin try to keep us from being children of God,
but Jesus conquered them when He grew up and died on the Cross.
When we put our trust in Jesus, He forgives our sin
and makes us children of God.

So it was a mighty thing that Jesus did when He came to earth—
no one else could have done it.
And yet, Jesus was born into the world as a tiny little baby,
just like you and me.

There was one difference, though.
Jesus was made in this special way:
There was no sperm from a father.
We call this the *Virgin Birth*,
because Mary was a virgin
when the baby Jesus began growing inside her.

The Bible tells us that Jesus was both man and God.

He was the Son of Mary, the Virgin Mother,
And the Son of God, the Heavenly Father.
But God knew all things, and He could foretell
That the Child would need a Father on earth as well.

So God looked down on earth for a Man
Whom He could trust to complete His plan;
A Man to adopt the Son of His love,
A Father to care for this Child from above.

God chose a Man
From a town called Nazareth,
A carpenter by trade
Whose name was Joseph.

God spoke to Him in a dream one night
and told him that Mary should be his Wife.
He loved her and brought her as Bride to his home,
And the Child that was born he raised as his own.

In Nazareth Jesus learned to play,
And as He grew up, He learned to obey.
He loved the Mother who gave Him birth,
And loved the Father who adopted Him on earth.

God wanted Jesus to have a father
who would love and take care of Him on earth.
Joseph already loved Mary.
God's angel told him about the miracle God had done in Mary,
and then Joseph knew that Mary should become his wife.
When Jesus was born,
Joseph adopted Him and became Jesus' earthly father.

**So Jesus was born in a wonderful way;
But, then—*so are we*, wouldn't you say?
For when God does *anything*, He does it well;
And that is the story we wanted to tell!**

Even though He was born in this very special way,
and was the Son of God,
Jesus had earthly parents to take care of Him
and raise Him when he was young—
Mary who had given Him birth,
and Joseph who had adopted Him.
He loved and obeyed them the way that God
wants all children to love and obey their parents.

The facts of Jesus' birth are different
than the facts of yours or mine.
But both ways are wonderful, aren't they?
In fact, all of God's ways are wonderful.
That's why we call this book...
THE WONDERFUL WAY THAT BABIES ARE MADE!